# PARADISE

A PHOTOGRAPHIC EXPLORATION OF
BRISBANE AND SOUTH EAST QUEENSLAND

BY NICK RAINS

To Janelle, my dear wife; without whose support, assistance and
tireless tripod-carrying this book would not have been possible.

To Irene.
Best Wishes
Nick Rains

Indian Head, Fraser Island

Designed by Artshak and Nick Rains.
Text by Nick Rains and Julietta Henderson.
All photography by Nick Rains.
Production by Ken Duncan Panographs Pty Ltd.
Printed in China by Everbest.

ISBN : 0-9752429-0-3
First Published 2004.

To see more of Nick's work visit:   **www.nickrains.com**

# PARADISE

## A PHOTOGRAPHIC EXPLORATION OF BRISBANE AND SOUTH EAST QUEENSLAND

### BY NICK RAINS

New Farm Park, Brisbane

# TABLE OF CONTENTS

Eagle Street Pier, Brisbane

# INTRODUCTION

A PHOTOGRAPHIC

EXPLORATION

OF SOUTH EAST

QUEENSLAND

BY NICK RAINS

Queensland - the Sunshine State – is renowned for its balmy tropical weather and relaxed lifestyle to match. The South East region of the state offers all the diversity of Queensland with the added advantages of its proximity to the colourful and cosmopolitan capital city of Brisbane.

The old adage of 'beautiful one day and perfect the next' certainly holds true of the South East. Mild winters and hot summers make it a popular destination with both domestic and international visitors looking to experience its famous hospitality and al fresco lifestyle.  From the endless beaches of the Gold and Sunshine Coasts to the lush sub-tropical rainforests of the hinterland, and the rolling countryside of the Darling Downs, it is possible to experience many of the state's best-known attractions within only a few hours travelling time from Brisbane.

The city of Brisbane easily keeps pace with its southern counterparts in terms of shopping and entertainment, while still managing to maintain its unique charm and hospitality. An extremely accessible city, Brisbane combines a progressive and creative city heart with a down to earth laid back attitude reflected in her many outdoor entertainment and parkland precincts. The cultural hub of South Bank is also home to a city beach, attracting visitors to the outdoor lagoon on the banks of the river, whilst the inner city Roma Street Parklands provide a lush and welcome respite from the bustling city.

The hinterland both north and south of Brisbane offers picturesque mountain villages, scenic drives, eclectic art and craft markets and miles of walking tracks through pristine National Parks. Within a short distance of these rainforest enclaves are the coastal regions of South East Queensland - hailed as amongst the best in the world. The huge sand islands of Fraser, Moreton and Stradbroke just off the coast attract visitors in droves to experience some of the most diverse wilderness areas of the country. Whilst these islands are undisputed tourism Mecca's, it is still possible to seek out regions of unpopulated beaches, amongst huge rolling sand dunes and dense pockets of sub tropical rainforests.

From the dazzling white beaches of Moreton Island and the massive shifting sand dunes on Fraser Island to the green jewelled hinterland and the millionaires' playgrounds of Noosa and the Gold Coast, South East Queensland truly offers something for everyone and deservedly earns the title - Paradise.

BRISBANE

City Hall, Brisbane

Story Bridge at dawn

Roma Street Gardens, a colourful oasis in the city

Brisbane Forest Park, ancient rainforest right on the edge of the city

The Graceful Tree Frog, part of Brisbane's abundant wildlife

Fireworks explode off the Victoria Bridge during the Riverfire Festival

Fireworks over the Treasury Casino

The afterburner from a RAAF F-111 jet lights up the city as the climax of the Riverfire Festival

Brisbane City as seen from Brisbane Lookout on Mount Coot-tha

The Brisbane River, the heart of the city

Eagle Street Markets

The Goodwill Bridge links South Bank with the Botanic Gardens

South Bank, an oasis in the city

The city skyline from the cliffs at Kangaroo Point

The business district near Eagle Street dwarfs some of
Brisbane's older buildings like Old St. Stephen's Church

Shorncliffe Pier at dawn

'Gooloowan' one of the many classic mansions in Ipswich, west of Brisbane

Old and New - west of Brisbane a replacement windmill pump stands tall over its predecessor

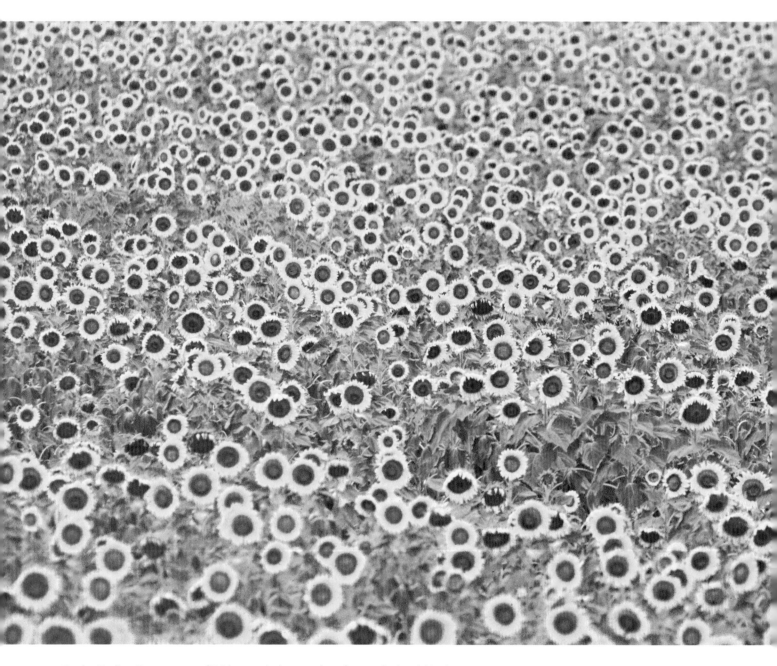

On the Darling Downs, west of Brisbane, whole seas of sunflowers flash gold in the summer sun

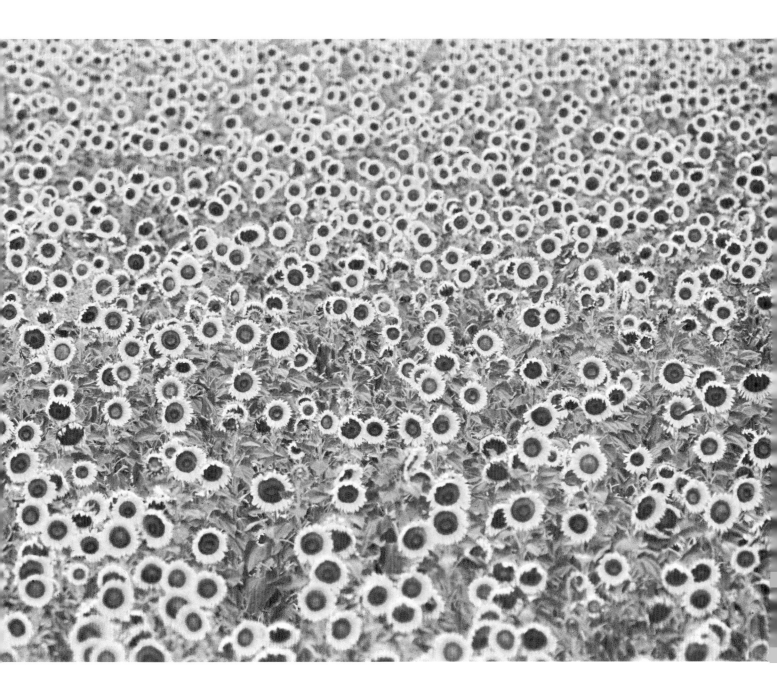

Samford Valley in the early morning light

BAY ISLANDS

North Stradbroke Island, Cylinder Beach at Point Lookout

Cape Moreton, at the northern tip of Moreton Island

Looking across to Moreton Island from Point Lookout on North Stradbroke Island

South Gorge, Point Lookout, North Stradbroke Island

Approaching storm, North Gorge, North Stradbroke Island

Frenchman's Beach,
North Stradbroke Island

Sunrise at North Gorge,
North Stradbroke Island

GOLD COAST

Sun and Surf - the Gold Coast has it all

Early morning strollers at Surfers Paradise

Greenmount Beach, Coolangatta

Dawn surfer, Mermaid Beach

Snapper Rocks at Point Danger

Strangler Fig, Tamborine National Park

North Tamborine

Natural Bridge National Park

Gwongarragong Falls, Lamington National Park

Purlingbrook Falls, Springbrook

Elabana Falls in the O'Reilly's section of Lamington National Park

SUNSHINE COAST

Lake Baroon, near Montville

Glasshouse Mountains from Mary Cairncross Lookout

Glasshouse Mountains from Bribie Island

The "Loo with a View" at Mooloolaba, dawn

Poet's Cafe, Montville

Eumundi Markets

Dicky Beach

Granite Bay, Noosa National Park.

FRASER ISLAND

Lake Mackenzie

Sunrise on the eastern coast

The wreck of the Maheno

Eli Creek

Pile Valley

Wangoolba Creek, Central Station

# IMAGE INDEX

**Page 8 - Jacarandas**
The Jacaranda Tree, for which Brisbane is renowned, flowers annually from October to December. The prolific blooms carpet the parks and avenues of the city transforming them into a sea of lavender. Newfarm Park and Graceville have excellent displays.

**Page 9 - City Hall**
King George Square is dominated by the clock on top of Brisbane City Hall, also home to the Museum of Brisbane. Brisbane maintains a vibrant city heart, with a thriving retail, arts and crafts community centered around Queen Street Mall.

**Page 10/11 - Story Bridge**
The Story Bridge is Brisbane's single most recognisable landmark and is the biggest steel cantilever bridge in Australia. It is situated just to the east of the city centre and links Kangaroo Point with the eastern CBD.

**Page 12/13 - Roma Steet Gardens**
Roma Street Parkland is the world's largest urban subtropical parkland. Its sixteen hectares encompass a network of pathways and gardens. Located adjacent to Roma Street Station, the parkland is within easy walking distance of the city centre.

**Page 14/15 - Brisbane Forest Park**
Only half an hour's drive from central Brisbane is a huge region of untouched rainforest threaded with trails and creeks. 10km NW of the city centre, Brisbane Forest Park HQ is on the Mount Nebo Road which continues from Waterworks Road.

**Page 16/17 - Brisbane Forest Park**
The pristine rainforest of Brisbane Forest Park is home to a great array of native wildlife like this Graceful Tree Frog, seen here calling during a light rain shower.

**Page 18 - Treasury Casino**
Converted out of the old Treasury Building, the Treasury Casino and adjoining hotel are a throwback to the Victorian days of grand architecture. The elaborate and classical exterior hides a state of the art casino. Located on the corner of George and Queen Streets.

**Page 19 - Riverfire Festival**
Every year during August and September Brisbane comes alive with the various River Festivals. 'Riverfire' is the most spectacular of these with huge fireworks displays launched from river barges, high rise offices and the Story Bridge. Best viewpoints are South Bank, Kangaroo Point and Bowen Terrace.

**Page 20/21 - Riverfire Festival**
The Riverfire Festival has one other ace up its sleeve. Some years, when available, the RAAF sends an F-111 fighter to do a flypast over the river. As it reaches the start of its run, the pilot ignites the afterburner and the plane heads for the sky on a huge fiery blast of light and noise.

**Page 22/23 - Brisbane Lookout**
At the summit of Mount Coot-tha, 7kms west of the CBD, as the crow flies, is the Brisbane Lookout with sensational views over the city to the Gateway Bridge and further to Moreton and Stradbroke Islands. Follow Milton Road west towards Toowong.

### Page 24/25 - Market and Boardwalk

The river is the heart of the city. On a Sunday the boardwalk is busy with joggers and the markets are in full swing. Operating from 8am until 4pm every Sunday, the Riverside and Eagle Street Markets are at the end of Charlotte Street, at Eagle Street Pier.

### Page 26/27 - Goodwill Bridge

The graceful curve of the Goodwill Bridge links Southbank Parklands to the city, and is the fourth crossing of the Brisbane River. Accessible only to pedestrians and cyclists, it was opened in 2001 and named in honour of the Goodwill Games held in the city that year.

### Page 28 - South Bank

The South Bank precinct was developed in 1988 for the World Expo and covers 17 hectares of riverfront. The lagoon is a hugely popular feature since it is just over the river from the city centre. Cross either the Victoria Bridge or the Goodwill Bridge to get there.

### Page 29 - South Bank

The Arbour is a bougainvillea covered walkway running the length of the South Bank gardens. On the weekends there are market stalls along the pathway and it makes for a pleasant shady walk in the summer.

### Page 30/31 - Brisbane City

One of the best views of the city is from Kangaroo Point cliffs where there are a series of lookouts along River Terrace. The best time is at dawn, as this image shows.

### Page 32 - Old St. Stephen's Church

Situated right next to St. Stephen's Cathedral on Elizabeth Street, this simple sandstone church was dedicated in 1850 and is Brisbane's oldest church.

### Page 33 - Business District

Huge glass towers dominate the eastern riverfront around Eagle Street. This is the financial and legal heart of the city, especially around the ends of Charlotte and Elizabeth Streets.

### Page 34/35 - Shorncliffe

Dawn at Shorncliffe Jetty, 21 kilometres NE of Brisbane CBD. Follow Sandgate Road out of the city, the jetty is off Park Parade in Shorncliffe.

### Page 36/37 - Ipswich

"Gooloowan" is a historic home in the heart of Ipswich, just off Warwick Road. Interested visitors should contact the Ipswich Tourism Information Centre to arrange a time to look around.

### Page 38/39 - Windmills

West of the residential areas of Brisbane, past Ipswich, are huge areas of rolling farmland and open pastures. Water pump windmills like these are a common sight out in the paddocks.

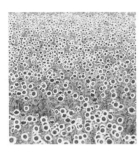

### Page 40/41 - Sunflowers

Huge fields of vivid yellow sunflowers put on a fabulous display in the summer months. They can be seen anywhere west of the Ranges, on the Darling Downs, about 100kms west of the city.

### Page 42 - Samford Valley

Samford Road heads NW out of the city and, out past Ferny Grove, runs into open rural areas. Samford Village is a quiet rural town only 20kms from the city centre and is surrounded by farms, fields and small lakes like this one in Samsonvale.

### Page 43 - Samford Valley

Brisbane is surrounded by rural areas and the Samford Valley is one of the closest. Follow Samford Road out of the city for 20kms and then take the Dayboro Road to find some delightful country scenery.

### Page 44 - Cylinder Beach

North Stradbroke Island, or 'Straddie' as the locals call it, is reached by ferry from Cleveland. Follow Old Cleveland Road out of town to get to the ferries. Bookings are essential in the holiday periods.

### Page 45 - North Stradbroke Island

'Straddie' has that holiday feel about it even though it is only a short distance from Brisbane. The beaches are superb and Cylinder Beach at Point Lookout must be one of the best along this part of the Queensland coastline.

### Page 46/47 - Moreton Island

Moreton Island is just to the north of Stradbroke Island and is more of a wilderness experience with most of the tracks being 4WD only. Ferries run from Scarborough to Bulwer. For the less adventurous, there is a resort at Tangalooma where wild dolphins come in to be fed daily.

### Page 48/49 - North Stradbroke Island

Blue water, pandanus palms, clean white sand - the epitome of a paradise and found only a short trip from Brisbane. Point Lookout, on the north coast of North Stradbroke Island, is the location for our book cover shot.

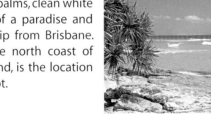

### Page 50/51 - South Gorge

Right next to the Surf Club at Point Lookout on North Stradbroke Island, South Gorge is a smaller version of North Gorge just to the west. There is a small sheltered beach accessible by a short footpath.

### Page 52/53 - North Gorge

Point Lookout is about 36km from Dunwich on North Stradbroke Island where the ferry drops off passengers and vehicles. Rocky Point, just to the east of the village has some spectacular coastline with short walking trails.

### Page 54 - North Gorge

This image was taken only 24 hours after the one on the preceding pages. From storm to glorious sunrise, the dawn is a great time to be up and about - you never know what you will see.

**Page 55 - Frenchman's Beach**
To the east of Cylinder Beach on North Stradbroke Island is the slightly more remote Frenchman's Beach, about 10 mins walk away. There is good surfing off the points and some good gutters for the keen fisherman.

**Page 56 - Coolangatta**
From the shore at Coolangatta the high rise apartments of Surfers Paradise can clearly be seen. There is excellent surfing here, Snapper Rocks is one of the best spots.

**Page 57 - Swimming Flags**
Queensland is serious about safe swimming and pairs of flags like this show the safest place to swim on the beach. Lifeguards keep watch between the flags here at Greenmount Beach in Coolangatta.

**Page 58/59 - Surfers Paradise**
Surfers Paradise is only one hour south of Brisbane and fronts endless golden beaches. The high rise apartments have incredible views over the ocean and up to South Stradbroke Island to the north.

**Page 60/61 - Greenmount Beach**
One of only 2 north facing beaches on the Gold Coast, Greenmount Beach is sheltered from the ocean swells so the beach itself is calmer and the rocky headland provides great surfing breaks. Head for Coolangatta, about 90 mins south of Brisbane on the main freeway.

**Page 62 - Mermaid Beach**
The Gold Coast is made up of many different beaches, all connected to make a vast strip of golden sand. Mermaid Beach, seen here at first light, is between Broadbeach and Miami Beach just to the south of Surfers Paradise itself.

**Page 63 - Snapper Rocks**
Better known for the surf break, Snapper Rocks is also a great place for a gentle swim when the conditions are calm. The water can be crystal clear like in this picture. Snapper Rocks is at the eastern end of Coolangatta, past Rainbow Beach.

**Page 64/65 - Mount Tamborine**
This tree is in the grip of a Strangler Fig which locks a tree in a network of vines. When the original tree dies, the vines remain, forming a complex latticework with a hollow centre. This example is in Tamborine National Park, turn right at the base of the stairs from the carpark.

**Page 66 - Mount Tamborine**
Away behind the glitter of the Gold Coast is the hinterland, a region of rolling countryside and some pristine rainforest like here in Tamborine National Park at North Tamborine. Turn off the Pacific Highway at Oxenford.

**Page 67 - North Tamborine**
The village of North Tamborine is nestled amongst the rainforest and the shops along the main street have all sorts of local arts and crafts on display. North Tamborine is 21km west of Oxenford.

### Page 68/69 - Natural Bridge

'Natural Arch' lies in the Numinbah Valley in Springbrook National Park. One hour inland from the Gold Coast on the New South Wales and Queensland border. Follow the Nerang River south west along Route 97 out of Nerang.

### Page 70 - Lamington National Park

Part of the World Heritage Central Eastern Rainforest Reserves since 1994. This is Gwongaragong Falls about 7km from the Binna Burra Lodge, on the Coomera Circuit Trail. Binna Burra is 10km from Beechmont, southwest of Nerang.

### Page 71 - Purlingbrook Falls

Springbrook National Park is another World Heritage Rainforest area, about 25km southwest of Mudgereeba on Route 99. Purlingbrook Falls, seen here, is one of Queensland's tallest single drop falls.

### Page 72 - Elabana Falls

Another Lamington National Park classic, Elabana Falls is only a 3km walk from O'Reilly's Guest House on the Box Forest Circuit. O'Reilly's Guesthouse is 36km from Canungra which is just to the west of Nerang on Route 90.

### Page 73 - Rainbow Lorikeet

O'Reilly's Guesthouse and gardens are famous for the prolific birdlife in the area. Clouds of Lorikeets, Rosellas and Parrots swirl around in a multicoloured explosion at feeding times.

### Page 74 - Alexandra Bay, Noosa

Noosa is well known for its up market shopping and fine dining. For those wishing to escape the bustle of the village however, Noosa National Park offers a diverse range of walking trails and some excellent beaches and bays. Walk north from Sunshine Beach, over a headland, to Alexandra Bay.

### Page 75 - Sunshine Beach

Sunshine Beach stretches as far as the eye can see towards Coolum and Maroochydore. This view is from the rocky headland at the northern end on the walking track to Alexandra Bay.

### Page 76/77 - Lake Baroon

Tucked out of sight behind Montville, Lake Baroon is a tranquil spot great for canoeing and fishing. Mist often fills the valley in the winter, as seen in this image. The lake is 2km west of Montville in the Sunshine Coast Hinterland.

### Page 78 - Glasshouse Mountains

Another famous landmark of the region, these volcanic plugs are about 60km north of Brisbane along the Bruce Highway. This view is from the Mary Cairncross Lookout, follow the Maleny Road out of Landsborough - it is signposted, turn left just before Maleny.

### Page 79 - Glasshouse Mountains

The setting sun lights up the clouds and the intense red is reflected in the waters of Pumicestone Passage. This view is from Bribie Island, about 23km east of Caboolture, north of Brisbane.

### Page 80t - Montville

The Hinterland of the Sunshine Coast is scattered with small villages like Flaxton, Mapleton, Maleny and Montville. All offer cafes, craft shops and sensational views over the coast towards Noosa and Coolum. Montville is southwest of Nambour, which is just off the Bruce Highway about 100kms north of Brisbane.

### Page 80b - Eumundi

The famous Eumundi Markets are held every Wednesday and Saturday. The historic hinterland village is fifteen minutes inland from Noosa on the Sunshine Coast and is a great place to browse arts, crafts and local produce.

### Page 82/83 - Mooloolaba

Just 10km off the Bruce Highway, almost exactly 100km from Brisbane, Mooloolaba is a very family oriented place where people from all over Australia come to enjoy the superb winter climate. The Esplanade offers a choice of cafes and shops and the sheltered beach is one of the best around.

### Page 81 - Montville

Arts and crafts are the main theme in Montville and the main street has shops offering a huge range of hand made items, as well as tea rooms, art galleries, antiques and novelties.

### Page 84/85 - Dicky Beach

Like the skeleton of a prehistoric creature, the ribs of the SS Dicky emerge from the sand of Dicky Beach at low tide. Dicky Beach is just north of Caloundra, 10km east of the Bruce Highway, turn off 82km north of Brisbane.

### Page 86 - Granite Bay

This is the furthest of the beaches from the centre of Noosa, and therefore the least crowded. In fact, on a weekday outside school holidays, the beach can be completely deserted and you can have the whole place to yourself. About 30 mins walk east of Noosa from the National Park carpark.

### Page 87 - Pebbles

Most of the beaches near Noosa feature these beautiful granite pebbles in many different colours and textures.

### Page 88 - Dingo

Dingos are a common sight on Fraser Island, but, like all wild animals, they should not be approached or fed. The Dingoes on Fraser are quite a pure strain as they have had less chance to interbreed with mainland dogs.

### Page 89 - Fraser Island

Dusk on the east coast of Fraser Island. This is the largest island on the east coast at 123km in length and is a World Heritage Site. The east coast is crossed by a series of small creeks; care must be taken whilst driving as they can erode into hard-to-see gutters to surprise the unwary.

### Page 90/91 - Lake Mackenzie

'Swimming pool blue' describes Lake Mackenzie well. The clean fresh water and white sand offer a sight that is hard to believe until you see it in reality. Lake Mackenzie is 8km north of Central Station via 4WD vehicle or as part of a guided tour.

### Page 92/93 - Fraser Island
Stormy dawn over the east coast of Fraser Island. Access to the island is by air or with a vehicle on a passenger barge (4WD only). Departs from Urangan (just out of Hervey Bay, 300 km north of Brisbane). There is another barge at Inskip Point just north of Noosa.

### Page 94/95 - Maheno
The wreck of the Maheno on Fraser Island. Located on Seventy-Five Mile Beach 3km north of Eli Creek. She was being towed to Japan for scrap in 1935 after serving in WW1 as a hospital ship when she lost rudder control in a cyclone and was swept ashore.

### Page 96/97 - Eli Creek
The largest creek on the eastern beach and a great place to drift down on a hot day. There is now a boardwalk to protect the bank and allow easy access for everyone. Eli Creek is 6km north of Happy Valley on the east coast.

### Page 98 - Fraser Island
The interior of Fraser Island is heavily wooded with some wonderful gnarly trunks like this tree on the way to the Knifeblade Sandblow, just inland from The Pinnacles, 11km north of Happy Valley.

### Page 99 - Pile Valley
So named after the huge trees which were once harvested for their rot resistant nature. Piles made from these trees were used in the Suez Canal. Logging ceased here years ago and these giants of nature dwarf the surrounding rainforest. Located just east of Central Station.

### Page 100/101 - Central Station
Wangoolba Creek runs through Central Station and is an abrupt change from the sand blows and beaches of the Island. Pure fresh water flows along a shallow creek past ancient Angiopteris ferns and Piccabeen palms. Central Station is 8km from where the ferry from River Heads, south of Urangan, drops off cars.

Mount Barney

# Photographic Notes

I have been photographing Australia's amazing scenery for almost 15 years and over that time I have used many different types of cameras. Each one will have its strengths and weaknesses just like any tool of the trade.

The most important thing is not the camera or the film but 'being there'. No camera will take photos for you and, as the old adage goes, the most important rule of photography is 'F8 and be there'.

Photography is all about timing and position. The best scenes are rendered average by poor light, thus by being in the right place at the right time you will increase your chances of finding good light, regardless of the camera you use. Like they say, 'location, location, location'.

The weather is a huge factor in photography but there is very little weather that is actually bad. A heavy overcast day is no good for beach shots but it is perfect for rainforest shots and, conversely, sunny days are not much good for rainforest images. Rain is temporary, and a clearing storm can reveal the most wonderful light. Many times I have sat through driving rain in the pre-dawn dark only to have the rain clear at dawn and provide me with a wonderful 'gift of light'.

Early starts are a necessary evil. I am not a morning person by nature but after dragging myself out of a warm bed at 4.00am and heading off into the dark I am constantly amazed at the rewards. There is always something to photograph in early morning light - it might not be what you were expecting but I am happy to submit to serendipity and take my good fortune where I find it.

On the subject of serendipity, I usually have a plan when I go off looking for images. I will know what I am looking for, I will have found out where I might find a certain sort of image and I will have checked the sunrise times as well as local maps to work out the best position and time for the image. My plans are not set in stone though, if my planned shot is not happening for whatever reason I do not wait around for hours, I judge the conditions and head for another location which might benefit, photographically speaking, from the prevailing conditions.

Like I said before, if I head for the beach and it's grey and cloudy I will often swap my plans around and look for some rainforest which always looks best under cloudy skies.

Regarding cameras, I use 3 main styles of camera. My primary camera is an EbonyRSW45 which is a modern 4x5 field camera fitted with a 6x12cm rollfilm back. I use 3 lenses, all Schneider - 58mmXL, 100mm and 150mm.

I have a collection of Canon 35mm bodies plus lenses from 17mm up to 600mm, all L-Series where possible.

However, more and more I am relying on a digital body, the D60, to replace my 35mm film shots. I love the flexibility of digital shooting and the files it produces are easily a match for scanned 35mm film. I even use this camera as a light meter when using the Ebony, its sophisticated matrix metering is hard to fool and I find it very effective at giving me the correct exposures for the film.

The other vital piece of gear is a sturdy tripod. All my 6x12 shots are taken with a tripod, and often the small format ones as well. Yes it's a pain to lug around but if you are going to a lot of trouble to get to a certain place then you owe it to yourself to get the highest quality images possible - and for that you absolutely need a good tripod. Mine is a Gitzo but any truly solid one will do.

Film is always Fuji Velvia100F. I love this stuff, it is sharp, with no reciprocity failure worth talking about, and it scans well. I am keen on digital but there is no competition - yet - with a well scanned 6x12 roll film transparency. I can do finely detailed prints up to 8 feet wide and beyond, something not possible on digital without a lot of expense and inconvenience. For me film rules - for the moment.

Happy shooting.

Nick Rains

# Rainspirit

*Australian Landscape Photography By Nick Rains*

Opened in 2002, the Rainspirit Gallery in central Brisbane is a stylish showcase for Nick's large format landscape work. Magnificent photographic prints up to 8 feet in length are on display and all are available for sale as ultimate quality Limited Edition Prints.

To step inside the Gallery is to experience all the wonderful scenery of Australia, all in one peaceful and welcoming environment.

**Rainspirit Gallery**
Level 1, 150 Queen Street, Brisbane, Qld 4000.
Ph: (07) 3210 2266
Fx: (07) 3210 6644
contact@rainspirit.com.au

# www.rainspirit.com.au

# Last Word

Brisbane is a terrific place to live and it has been my priviledge to be able to show the world some of the wonderful places within 2 hours drive of my home.

I would like to sincerely thank the following people who have been involved with this book project in various ways.

Ken Duncan and Janet Gough whose input and feedback has been much appreciated. Councillor David Hinchliffe, Deputy Mayor of Brisbane, whose support in the very early stages of the project proved invaluable. Andrew Sivijs, Brisbane City Council Economic Development, for his help in organising the Council's generous support. Stephanie Strange, Chris and Steve Hunt and Janelle Lugge for proof reading. Julietta Henderson for researching the Photo Index section. Jess and Shelley of Artshak for coming up with the original design concepts. Last, but by no means least, Jacques Guerinet of Fuji Australia for supplying me with plenty of my favourite film

*Dedicated to a better Brisbane*